What Is Marxism All About?

Written by Fight Imperialism - Stand Together
(FIST) members: Tyneisha Bowens, Ben
Carroll, LeiLani Dowell, Elena Everett,
Julie Fry, Larry Hales, David Hoskins, Caleb
Maupin, and Dante Strobino

World View Forum

What Is Marxism All About?

Authors: Tyneisha Bowens, Ben Carroll, LeiLani Dowell, Elena Everett, Julie Fry, Larry Hales, David Hoskins, Caleb Maupin, and Dante Strobino

First copyright 1974

Edited by LeiLani Dowell and David Hoskins

Reprinted October 2009

ISBN: 9780895671530

Revised: June 2009

Library of Congress Control Number: 2009939894

Cover art by Mike Martinez, Original artwork by Tom Spence, Art work and design by Mike Martinez

Produced by Dante Strobino

Published by
World View Forum
55 West 17 St, 5C
New York, NY 10011

Table of Contents

Introduction

This pamphlet is a republication of an earlier work by the same ti-
tle. That work was based on a series of articles that appeared in Workers World newspaper in 1974 and 1975, entitled "What We Mean By."
Each chapter strives to explain and illustrate Marxist terminology in
intelligent, but non-technical, language.

Readers will find terms like socialism, imperialism, and self-determination described in the pages that follow. The Marxist definitions
of these words help to sharpen an understanding of society from a
working-class perspective.

Karl Marx was a philosopher, a sociologist before sociology even
existed, a historian, an economist and a political scientist. Marx ex-
amined society from many different angles. He studied the world, nature and history, and began to discover the laws that govern societal
and economic evolution. Just as Charles Darwin discovered the way
nature adapts and changes over time, Marx discovered and extensive-
ly documented how societies adapt and change over time, and the

laws that govern that change.

Marx was more than a thinker or an academic. He was also an activist. The concepts in this pamphlet will help 21st century activists organize for the radical and transformative change that Marxists call revolution.

Workers World Party, a multinational, working class, anti-racist, anti-sexist, anti-homophobic, and revolutionary Marxist-Leninist party, was founded on the principles and ideas first laid out by Marx many years ago, as well as many other great revolutionaries since his time. This pamphlet is being revised and republished by Fight Imperialism, Stand Together (FIST), an autonomous youth and student organization affiliated with Workers World Party on the basis of solidarity and a shared revolutionary socialist perspective.

The republication is the work of the many great FIST writers who contributed to rewriting this work--Tyneisha Bowens, Ben Carroll, LeiLani Dowell, Elena Everett, Julie Fry, Larry Hales, David Hoskins, Caleb Maupin and Dante Strobino. Mike Martinez and Jon Regis designed new chapter artwork and helped reproduce the artwork from the original publication. Mike Martinez designed the cover art. Tom Spence created the original artwork The chapters were edited by LeiLani Dowell and David Hoskins. Technical editing was performed by Dante Strobino. Of course, the republication itself would not be possible without the work of those Workers World writers in 1974 and 1975: Lorraine Breslow, Naomi Cohen, Bill Del Vecchio, Bob Dobrow, Deirdre Griswold, Bob McCubbin, Elizabeth Ross, Sharon Shelton and Andy Stapp.

Class Society

"The workers have nothing to lose but their chains." "The history of all hitherto existing society is the history of class struggles." "Workers [and oppressed] of the world unite!"

These are just a few of the slogans still in use today that Karl Marx and Frederick Engels first popularized in 1848 when they wrote "The Communist Manifesto." These popular slogans, and the class society they describe, are just as relevant today as when they were first written more than 150 years ago.

"The Communist Manifesto" describes the process by which society developed over time so that today it is divided into roughly two great classes. Marxists often refer to the ruling class as the bourgeoisie and the working class as the proletariat. Each class is defined by its relationship to the major means of production.

The ruling class makes up a tiny minority of society. This class owns all the property of industry and commerce--the factories, banks, telecommunication companies, retail stores and more. Most politicians in capitalist democracy are either direct members of the ruling class or its hired agents. Managers, police officers, judges and corporate newspaper editors are also ruling class agents. The ruling class makes its profits by exploiting the labor of the working class. These capitalists see money as a means to make more money and increase their power. The money reinvested to make more money is called capital.

The ruling class is a small bunch. Many of their names are easily recognized. Warren Buffet, Rupert Murdoch, Michael Bloomberg, Bill Gates, and the Walton family (owners of Wal-Mart) are just a few of the biggest names in modern capitalism. These five names alone had a net worth that exceeded $220 billion in 2008.

The working class includes all the people who create all the goods and services in capitalist society. These workers make the vast bulk of their income by working for someone else. A person is still a member of the working class even if their income is supplemented by investments in their 401K or stock options that the company provides its employees in lieu of direct wages.

The unemployed are also workers. Unemployment is a constant and necessary feature of capitalism. The ruling class purposefully forces a significant number of workers into unemployment as a reserve army to compete with employed workers and force down wages. The reserve army also provides the capitalist with the flexibility to rapidly hire these unemployed workers at low wages during periods of economic expansion.

Stay-at-home parents are also members of the working class. Their unpaid labor is necessary to raise the next generation of workers for exploitation by the bosses. Children are workers' dependents who are being brought up and trained to be future workers. The children of workers are members of the working class.

The working class is an international class that is artificially divided into separate countries because of the history of capitalist rule. The U.S. working class is multinational. A large portion of the workers here belong to oppressed Black, Latina/o, Asian, Native and Arab nationalities. Some are immigrants and may be documented or not. Workers from the oppressed nationalities, including documented and undocumented immigrants, form a super-exploited segment of the working class. One thing all workers have in common is that their labor produces all the wealth in society.

Capital and Capitalism

In every society, from ancient times to feudalism and in modern capitalist society, it has been the labor of human beings that sustains the society and creates wealth. It is this basic fact and the acknowledgment of the laborers as a class in bourgeois capitalist society that has been obscured to many in the U.S.

The history of modern society is the history of two antagonistic camps: the exploited class, the workers, and the exploiting class, the bourgeoisie.

Some may characterize this current period in history as "capitalism gone wild." But the system of capitalism hasn't just gone off the track. Its objective reality is simply playing out in all its ruthlessness.

As Karl Marx said, capitalism came into the world "dripping from head to toe from every pore with blood and dirt." It was the urban middle class, including shopkeepers and merchants, desiring free markets and democratic rights, religious freedom and other freedoms not granted under the absolute monarchies of Europe, who

3

would become the new rulers under capitalist society.

Numerous European states had already engorged themselves by plundering Asia, Africa and the Americas through mass murder, genocide and the enslavement of the peoples of these lands. Marx called this "the primitive accumulation of capital." It is described as such because of its savage brutality and utter disregard for humanity.

That period of history--where certain European states garnered great wealth, the likes of which had not previously been seen, and developed their societies from this wealth--was unprecedented at the time.

Never had humanity seen such brutality. The colonization of the Americas--done mostly through blunt force--and the enslavement of mostly African people on huge plantations in the Americas filled the coffers of these European states. And while the European states were in competition with one another for riches, they were united in the view of their superiority over the darker people of the planet.

In class society, wealth is concentrated in the hands of a few, while the majority of people are exploited for their labor. It is human labor that sustained pre-class human beings and, as previously mentioned, produces all wealth in class society.

All class society is characterized by exploitation--whether under feudalism, where serfs, working on land owned by lords, surrendered the fruit of their labor to the lords in exchange for living on the land and keeping enough to feed their families; or under semi-feudal chattel slave conditions in the U.S., where enslaved Africans had no rights and all they produced belonged to the master.

While bourgeois capitalist society may have done away with the feudal society that preceded it and has allowed for what seems to be more individual freedom and democracy, it is still based on exploitation.

The capitalist class owns all the means of production in society: the machinery, factories, and raw materials. It gets its wealth by the labor of the workers—who sustain themselves and survive by selling their labor to the owners.

This new wage system is nothing more than a different sort of enslavement. The rulers or owners gain huge profits off the backs of workers. The worker has no ownership over the fruit of labor and, like the other resources used to produce things, belongs to the owner for the amount of time the worker's labor is purchased. The thing produced is then turned around and sold back to the worker at an inflated price.

Rulers in capitalist society may exploit in different ways, but the reason is the same: riches and profit. The interests and needs of the workers and rulers are diametrically opposed.

Exploitation and Surplus Value

Human labor is a commodity—a thing of value. It is also a value that, when used, creates value. It is from the labor of the worker that the owner derives profit. If a worker is slated to work eight hours, a small percentage of that time is spent covering the cost of the worker's wage. The rest of the time is unpaid labor—surplus labor—and it is from this that the owner gains extra or surplus value.

All that extra time, the worker gets nothing and the owner reaps all the benefits. The owners do everything necessary to increase the flow of profit: they fire workers, while expecting those who remain to increase productivity; they decrease benefits; they set workers in competition with one another, a process which drives down wages. All these things cause misery for the workers but are designed to increase profit. That profit is dispersed amongst the owners and the high-end managers, but not amongst the workers who create it.

How many times has a company announced layoffs, all while CEO types get bonuses or raises for "tightening the belt"? A good example is that of Circuit City, which in early 2007 had 46,000 workers in Canada and the U.S.

In April of 2007, Circuit City, the second-largest electronic retailer in the U.S., decided to lay off 3,400 workers because they were "being paid too much." The company did this because it had only an 8 percent growth in sales in the previous quarter, and sales were forecasted to grow to only 10 percent in the next quarter.

While Circuit City started off paying workers merely $7.75 an hour and its average employee made only $10 an hour, it stated that its chief rival paid its workers less on average and that it could not compete while paying an average wage that translates to just $19,200 per year before taxes. The poverty threshold in the U.S. for a family of three in 2006 was a little more than $16,000 before taxes.

The workers were told they could reapply for their jobs at lower pay. But the CEO of Circuit City continued to receive $8.52 million, including a $975,000 salary, a year. Upon news of the layoffs, the stock value of the company rose 1.9 percent.

Millions of people around the world go hungry and lack access to clean water, health care, adequate housing, clothing and transportation. Yet so much goes to waste in the so-called developed world.

Factories close; companies go belly-up as each capitalist tries to outdo the other and in the process they produce and produce. As their unplanned, anarchic production leads to a crisis of overproduction they transfer the crisis to the workers, with pay cuts, mass layoffs and firings. This boom-or-bust reality is because of the nature of the system, which is to reap greater and greater profits regardless of what is actually needed.

In times of crisis, the capitalists need new markets, cheaper access to resources and new, cheaper, easily exploitable labor. This fuels the drive to war.

If one were to add the expense of war--both in monetary and more tragic human loss--the waste makes even less sense.

The Pentagon budget alone for fiscal year 2008 was $470 billion. This does not account for the billions spent on the U.S. imperial military adventures in Iraq and Afghanistan. Hundreds of thousands of Iraqi and Afghan people, and thousands of young women and men drawn into the U.S. military, have been killed and maimed.

But what is the answer? The answer is the abolition of the capitalist system and the expropriation of the capitalist class. In the place of the capitalist system a system based on actual human need, in solidarity with the oppressed and workers the world over, needs to be built. The system of socialism removes the profit motive; the means of production are held and developed by the entire society for the need of all in society, not for profit.

It is through this system that problems as they come are dealt with, as it is through need and solidarity that problems are solved, not through profit.

Private Property

Private property, to a communist, is not your shoes or toothbrush, or even your house.

Those things are called personal property and under socialism and under communism they continue to belong to workers in much the same manner they do now.

When Marxists speak of private property under capitalism, it refers to the tools of production that should be owned by all of society, such as factories, lands, stores, mines, and all those things that are gifts of nature or are built by many people over many centuries, but are now being monopolized by a few. These few don't concern themselves with how many years of human labor went into their creation, just so long as they alone can reap profits from legal ownership of that property.

The goal of socialism is to increase personal property many times over, through the abolishment of private property.

Enemies of communism say that communists want to take small

farms away from the women and men who worked so hard to keep them going for so many years and put small grocers, tailors and carpenters out of business and deny them an independent living.

Capitalism has already put most of these small operators out of business and made wage slaves of them, destroying their dreams of independent prosperity. Wal-Mart and Target routinely put small retailers out of business. Giant agribusiness conglomerates mow down small farms every week. Supermarket chains have wiped out the corner grocer; and corporate bookstores like Barnes & Noble and Borders are responsible for the destruction of small book shops. The few small businesses that remain live precariously on the edge of an abyss, with whole families sometimes working long hours to compete.

Private property in the means of production is owned by a very small fraction of the population in the capitalist countries, but it was produced by generations of working people--by the immense majority who, over the centuries, learned to till the soil, mine the ores, and make buildings and bridges out of trees, rock, clay and new combinations of nature's bounty.

In the earliest days of capitalist accumulation there were, here and there, some people who amassed relatively small private properties through hard work and miserly living. But most properties, even then, were gained through influence, bribery and deceit--by robbing the working poor of their labor. It is laughable to think that anyone or any family could have earned a billion dollars--or even a million--without becoming themselves a big capitalist and utilizing mass exploitation of labor.

Personal property has increased in the capitalist world, too: vast estates, mansions, yachts, private jets, designer clothes all are hoarded by the few, while the personal property of the many decreases in quantity and quality. The 2007 housing bubble bust caused the greatest loss of personal wealth in history for working people in the United States as millions lost their homes. What they had thought of as theirs belonged, under capitalist law, to the banks and mortgage companies, which snatched it away from them.

In the struggle to secure personal property--the necessities and comforts of life--the working class will find it necessary to overthrow the institution of private property and put all the means of production under the control of a workers' government.

In some places the people have overthrown the system of private property; in many others the people are working towards its abolition. Now, with the international capitalist class in a huge economic and financial crisis, more and more workers and oppressed people are saying "enough is enough." Rebellions are taking place across the world, from industrial centers to former colonies.

Personal property--homes, nourishing food, cameras, bicycles, books and thousands of small items that raise the health and cultural level of a people--will increase year by year under socialism, but no one will personally own land, the factories, or the banks.

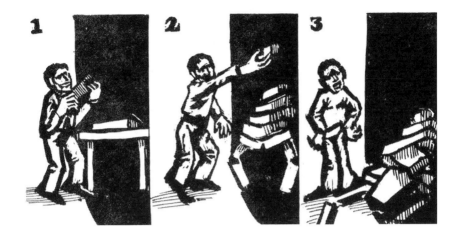

Dialectical and Historical Materialism

As part of their socialization within class society, workers are encouraged to believe that individual self-interest is the foundation of human nature and survival. If this is true, all of human history has been a struggle driven by greed. Workers are told that society cannot be changed because of "natural" human greed. Workers are given the option of either giving in to that greed or using religion or mysticism to "rise above the material world."

Neither of those options provides a realistic alternative or solution to the problems presented by class society. Marxists understand that society has not always been driven by individual self-interest and greed, that greed is not a part of human nature, and that society can be changed for the better. All of this can be demonstrated by using dialectical materialism, a scientific method of thinking to evaluate the world in which humans live.

Dialectical materialism can be broken down into its respective components for a better understanding. Dialectics describes the scientific method Marxists use to analyze the world around them. Materialism represents Marxists' conception of the reality dialectics is intended to analyze.

Dialectics, as a method of analysis, takes into account the interconnectedness of nature, the contradictions and state of continuous change inherent in it, and the process by which natural quantitative change leads to qualitative change. Simply put, dialectics holds that all things are in a constant state of change, that this continual change is a result of interactions and conflicts, and that many small hidden changes add up until the thing in question has been qualitatively transformed into something different. The process by which water is transformed into steam, by heating it until it passes the boiling point, illustrates the concept of dialectics at work.

Materialism is the Marxist conception of nature as it exists without any supernatural or mystical dimension. Materialism holds that objective reality exists independent of human consciousness and that matter is primary.

Dialectical materialism shows that people's thoughts, characters and actions are shaped by the conditions in the world around them, the material world. When people look at the world through the lens of dialectical materialism they can see the logical development of beliefs and thoughts, actions and events, and even human history as a whole.

Historical materialism extends the principles of dialectical materialism to the study of society and its history. Historical materialism recognizes that history and society develop based on material, economic conditions. Therefore all development, that of ideas and that of institutions, is based on conflicts and interactions in the material world.

This understanding of development and change refutes the argument that class society is based on natural human greed. The development of class society came from the material interactions and conflicts that humans have faced over history.

A belief in dialectical materialism does not validate the oppression and exploitation of the working masses within this development of class society. Marxists argue that this scientific view analyzes how humanity and society have developed so that it can be changed. Most importantly, it instills the knowledge of human agency in history-- that people are in fact able to change the oppressive society that they live in, and that society cannot possibly stay the same as the material world changes. Dialectical materialism implies that capitalism, like everything else, has a birth, a development, and will have an end.

Class Solidarity and the Class Struggle

One of the greatest weapons that workers and oppressed people possess against the bosses and capitalists is our unity. When Marxists speak or write about proletarian solidarity, working class solidarity and international solidarity, they mean the complete unity of interest of all the peoples oppressed and exploited by capitalism. It is only by coming together in solidarity--it is only through closing ranks against the common enemy--that any victory has ever been won by the masses of people.

Working-class solidarity is present in every picket, every union action, every strike and any time workers take a stand against the bosses. If workers go on strike, only a scab or a boss will cross the picket line, while all workers who feel solidarity with each other refuse. Workers formed trade unions and continue to organize into unions today out of the knowledge that only through banding together in solidarity can even the slightest improvement be gained in working conditions, wages, job security, and so forth. Whenever a struggle breaks out, workers in unions and other progressive people from the community will come to the aid and defense of the workers who have gone out on strike, occupied their factory, or taken other decisive action, in order to strengthen the class struggle against the bosses. This solidarity of the workers is the capitalists' biggest threat.

The bosses attempt to break up and destroy working-class solidarity by dividing the poor and working people against each other. They use sexism to turn men against women workers. They try to break the multinational unity of the working class by dividing white workers and people of color, and further attempt to pit Black and Brown workers against one another. Using xenophobic hysteria, bosses attempt to turn U.S.-born workers against immigrant workers. Bosses will also try to divide straight and lesbian, gay, bi, trans and queer (LGBTQ) workers.

Nonetheless, the solidarity of the world working class and oppressed peoples has often defeated the attempts of the capitalist to trick working people into fighting against one another.

U.S. workers showed solidarity with the people of Iraq fighting against U.S. imperialism when, on May Day 2008, workers from the International Longshore and Warehouse Union went on strike to protest the war on Iraq. Similarly, Greek longshore workers blocked a shipment of U.S. arms and munitions to Israel during the U.S.-Israeli siege on Gaza in early 2009.

The boycott of Mt. Olive pickles by millions of people in the U.S. who support the Farm Labor Organizing Committee, when workers were struggling for higher wages and better working conditions, is an act of working-class solidarity.

Real working-class solidarity can only be achieved, and real unity won, when solidarity is based on the liberation of all people from the shackles of capitalist society. This means, for example, that male workers must actively fight against sexism and for the rights of women workers; white workers must struggle against racism and national oppression, and for the full rights of Black and Brown workers.

Workers need class solidarity that unites with the struggles for national liberation, women's liberation, LGBTQ liberation, and the struggles of immigrant workers for full rights, to win the liberation of all oppressed and exploited by capitalism through the worldwide socialist revolution. This is the greatest act of working class solidarity and is the only thing that will bring an end to the capitalist system of profit and exploitation once and for all, and that will ultimately wipe out all oppression. There can be no class struggle without class solidarity.

Imperialism and Globalization

Television viewers can turn on any news channel almost any time of day and within moments images of war will spring across the screen. Images of ground troops in Iraq, U.S. military bases in Korea, and air raids in Afghanistan are complemented by the voices of somber newscasters warning about the potential of a naval blockade against Iran or political and humanitarian crises in places like Zimbabwe and Darfur. The corporate media and its talking heads throw out routine phrases like "national security," "war on terror," and "Islamic fundamentalism" in an attempt to explain away these pictures of crisis and conflict.

The real root of all this conflict can be found in the nature of imperialism and the role it plays on the international stage. Imperialism is the final stage of capitalism that is reached when the capitalists of a particular country are compelled to economically expand beyond their own borders through military force or other methods of coercion. Imperialism is referred to as the highest stage of capitalism because the capitalist system must either expand or die in its quest to accumulate profits.

Vladimir Lenin was a leader of the 1917 Bolshevik Revolution in Russia and a prominent Marxist who popularized the term imperialism and provided it with a scientific definition. Lenin identifies five essential features of imperialism in his germinal work on the subject, "Imperialism: The Highest Stage of Capitalism." The five features of imperialism are:

1) The creation of decisive monopolies through the concentration of production and capital.
2) The merger of bank capital and industrial capital to create an oligarchy of financial capital.
3) The export of capital and commodities, with capital being the more fundamental of the two.
4) The formation of global capitalist monopolies which share the world among themselves.
5) The territorial division of the whole world amongst the most powerful capitalist powers.

These five features of imperialism explain the process by which monopoly capitalism has developed to the point where it raises huge armies and navies and develops high-tech weapons of mass destruction in order to forcibly open new markets and exploit new sources of cheap labor. It is this character of imperialism--its nature to carve the world up for the great capitalist powers--that is behind all the images of war and devastation on the nightly news.

Wars have historically been waged by imperialist powers, regardless of the type of political administration. Liberal or conservative, social democratic or monarchist or fascist, governments of imperialist countries have all been responsible for waging imperialist war. Capitalism's expand-or-die dilemma requires near constant war, regardless of the politics of the government in power. Fred Goldstein, a leader of Workers World Party, examines the three stages of imperialist war throughout history in his book, "Low-Wage Capitalism."

The first stage of imperialist war was to redivide the world. This stage was marked by conflict among the imperialist powers to carve out their respective spheres of influence. This method of imperialist war lasted until the end of the Second World War, which brought about the defeat of German, Italian and Japanese imperialism; severely diminished the capacity of Britain and France; and positioned the U.S. as the dominant imperialist power. The war also ended with the Soviet Union's historic victory over fascism and the defeat of the German Nazi armies. This new dynamic--U.S. imperialist dominance and the emergence of the Soviet Union as a socialist superpower--led to the second stage of imperialist war: war between the socialist and imperialist camps.

This stage of imperialist war was marked by a nuclear-armed U.S. and its mobilization of all the capitalist forces to contain the twin threats to imperialism at the time--socialist revolutions and national liberation struggles. The inter-imperialist struggle to redivide the globe was replaced by a struggle between the competing social systems of socialism and capitalism. The Korean War, the Vietnam War, the Bay of Pigs invasion of Cuba, and the CIA dirty wars in Angola, Nicaragua and El Salvador are all examples of the imperialist war against socialism and national liberation during this period.

The third and current stage of imperialist war was ushered in after the 1991 defeat of the Soviet Union. This stage has been marked by war for global reconquest of the former socialist camp countries and of countries led by independent bourgeois-nationalist governments that the Soviet Union had supported. Expansion of NATO into the former socialist-bloc countries of Europe and the U.S.-led NATO war against Yugoslavia exemplify imperialism's drive for global reconquest.

Today, the word globalization is commonly used to describe the same phenomenon that Lenin explained more than 100 years ago. Bosses and bourgeois politicians talk about globalization as if it is a new and benign form of capitalism that peacefully spreads wealth and stability to poor countries around the world. But the truth is that what the mainstream media calls globalization is just a modern form of imperialism. Now, instead of colonizing oppressed countries through the brute force of imperialist armies alone, bankers and corporations use institutions like the World Bank and the International Monetary Fund to help coerce those countries into bending to their will.

And those who try to resist globalization still face the threat of imperialist war. More than a million people were killed by the U.S.-led imperialist coalition against Iraq after Iraq's leaders dared to nationalize their own oil fields and use their resources for the independent development of their own country. Today in Venezuela, that country's democratically elected president, Hugo Chávez, faces the constant threat of imperialist invasion for speaking out against the global capitalist monopolies and using his country's resources for Venezuela's people.

The truth is that what capitalists call globalization is just an expansion of imperialism. No matter what the bosses and the politicians call it, the modern expansion of capitalism is just as brutal and miserable for the workers and oppressed of the world as ever. Globalization has plunged hundreds of millions of people around the globe into desperate poverty. And although the bosses talk about the modern "peaceful" expansion of capitalism, the reality is that the U.S. alone has been at war almost every year since the fall of the Soviet Union and has caused the deaths and injuries of millions in imperialist wars since the term "globalization" was popularized.

Imperialism is the enemy of the entire global working class. It does not matter if workers live inside an imperialist country or outside its borders--imperialism is their class adversary. Workers living in the exploiting countries have a special obligation to support workers in the countries exploited by imperialism as they fight to liberate themselves.

Women's Oppression

The oppression of women in the 21st century is perhaps more multi-faceted and developed than it has been historically. Gains in women's rights have been products of the protracted struggle of women and anti-sexist allies over the centuries, but these gains have not ended the oppression of women.

On average women make about 30 percent less than what men make for the same job, hours and skill level. Women of color make even less on average than white women. This evident economic discrimination is just one part of the systematic oppression of women.

For centuries the labor of women has been devalued and exploited through lesser or no wages; unsafe and unregulated working conditions; the nonpayment for extensive and valuable domestic work; and being forced to give all wages to one's father or male spouse. The "glass ceiling"--limits placed on the upward mobility of women in the workforce--traps women in low-wage industries.

Since women are paid less than men but take up the bulk of the domestic work in the home, women are oftentimes trapped into economic dependence on men or are forced to rely on a sexist system for economic help. This assistance is very under-funded and does little to aid women in economic need.

In some instances women are forced to enter into sex work--an extra-legal system of sexual and economic exploitation. Currently women make up the bulk of the poor and are most affected by economic crises; this is the "feminization of poverty."

Women's oppression is evident in the political arena as well. Capitalist politics have historically disenfranchised women by allowing only men to vote and hold public office. The women's suffrage moment of the late 19th and early 20th centuries obtained the right to vote for women, but women's roles in politics are often still limited to the appearance-making spouse of a political candidate. Even women who have had some level of success entering the political arena have had to adhere to the rules and expectations of a male-dominated political system. Women are still vastly outnumbered on the Supreme Court and in the U.S. Congress, which for more than 85 years has failed to pass a simple Equal Rights Amendment.

The oppression of women is based in the historical status of women as private property, and their unequal relationship to men in the institution of family. Legislation upholding the status of women as property still exists today. These laws limit the self-determination of women by placing boundaries on their sexualities and their bodies. Though some reproductive rights, like abortion and birth control, are legal for most women in the U.S., the right to abortion and birth control are still legally and extra-legally restricted to many women and often times these rights are out of the economic reach of working and poor women. These rights, which were fought for by generations of women and allies, are now under attack. Many states are successfully passing legislation to severely restrict abortion and other methods of birth control.

It is hard to see how in this system women could ever obtain true reproductive justice--meaning not just the right to choose to reproduce, but the right to bear children into a society that will ensure that child is well-fed, clothed, sheltered and educated.

When discussing women's oppression it is easy for people to ignore the social and cultural manifestations of women's oppression. The cultural manifestations include the sexual degradation and overall sexualization of women in popular culture; the association of women with products that can be bought and sold; the normalization of abusive behavior towards women; and the classification of women as intellectually and physically inferior and submissive to men. These aspects of women's cultural oppression are reinforced through popular television programs and commercials; popular music and music videos; pornography; magazines and other forms of advertisement.

Women are stereotyped in the media as sexual objects that men can obtain through monetary or material exchange. These images of women, which are by far the most prevalent images of women in all popular forms of entertainment and advertising, encourage men to mimic these sexist views in their social interactions with women. Women are also encouraged to fit into these stereotypes and discouraged from taking active and independent roles in defining their sexualities, body image and social interactions.

One may ask, when faced with the historical and current oppression of women, "Was it always like this?" The answer is no. Though women have been oppressed and exploited for centuries, this sexist hierarchy was not always the case. During the majority of human history women were not oppressed. In fact, in the old communal societies women were equal to men. In some instances, matriarchal societies existed. It is important to note that in these societies men were not oppressed by women, but women held a certain social and cultural importance to the family and community that was not based on the exploitation or oppression of men.

While the division of labor (social roles that men and women fulfilled) was different, there was no system of inferiority or superiority based on the division of labor. Not until the emergence of private property, and therefore class society, did the oppression of women emerge. Since then women have been oppressed in all forms of class society including slavery, feudalism, and capitalism. It is easy to conclude that women's oppression is historically based in class oppression and is currently perpetuated by class society.

Marxists argue that the absence of women's oppression in pre-private-property societies proves that women's oppression is based on the system of private property and not a natural outgrowth of male dominance over women. Consequently, the abolition of private property will lay the basis for the complete liberation of women.

Racism and
Oppressed Nations

In an open colonial relationship, it is easy to recognize an oppressed nation. The Irish people, for example, have been oppressed by England for centuries and during most of that time denied the rights of nationhood.

Generally, oppressed nations have consisted of people sharing a common language, territory, and culture, and a common oppression. In Puerto Rico, for example, not only do the first three characteristics apply, but the Puerto Rican independence movement has waged a brave liberation struggle in Puerto Rico, and within the United States itself, against U.S. occupation of the island.

Imperialism, however, has complicated the definition of an oppressed nation by moving whole peoples from their original geographical locations and breaking down language and cultural differences.

In the U.S. there are still oppressed nations who are systematically singled out for oppression, regardless of where they live, because of their ethnic and historical backgrounds.

Thus we say that the U.S. today is multinational, with a dominant white nation alongside and intermingled with a number of oppressed national groupings, including the Black, Latina/o, Asian and Pacific Islander, and Native nations.

The working class too is multinational. At the factories and in the shops, workers of different nations work side-by-side. But the entire working class is exploited by the same capitalist class--the bankers, the big farmers or agribusinesses, the industrialists, and the landlords--and this capitalist class belongs primarily to the upper strata of the dominant white nation.

How did it come to be this way? Why did people coming to the U.S. from different European nations in the early days become assimilated, while those who originally inhabited this continent, those forcibly brought from Africa, and others have remained oppressed?

The European immigrants to North America, while some were rich and some poor, were gradually assimilated, their national differences (though not necessarily their class differences) breaking down to where they now constitute a nation in themselves. The majority of them chose to come to the U.S. because of economic and political conditions in their own countries.

But as U.S. capitalism developed and the 13 colonies won their independence, the U.S. forcibly conquered other nations and nationalities and took them over through military expansionist wars. The Native nations, Puerto Rico, Hawaii and Aztlan (the southwest area of the U.S. that was stolen from Mexico) are a few examples. In addition, entire peoples were uprooted from their African homelands and kidnapped to the U.S. through the slave trade.

The U.S., as the world's biggest superpower, has also forced economic policies onto so-called "developing" countries that have had a devastating impact on the people of those countries. As a result, many workers migrate to the U.S. in search of job opportunities. These national groupings of immigrants are then forced into the lowest-paying, super-exploitative jobs in the U.S. and live in fear of workplace raids, detention and deportation.

All these different oppressed nations and nationalities have been retained within the boundaries of the U.S., their lands stolen and plundered of natural resources, their people used as a source of cheap labor. Because of slavery and imperialist intervention, they were prevented from developing as independent nations. Nor have they received the protection of the democratic rights supposedly granted by the U.S. Constitution.

In reality these oppressed people are internal colonies of the U.S. ruling class.

The capitalist ruling class has deliberately fostered divisions between white workers and oppressed peoples. This divide-and-conquer tactic means denying oppressed people their democratic rights; miseducating white workers and attempting to indoctrinate them with racist ideas; blaming nonwhites for the evils of capitalism; giving white workers a few extra crumbs (while still exploiting their labor intensively); and creating a system of racism and national oppression based on super-exploitation, inequality and prejudice.

LGBTQ Oppression

Until recent times, lesbians, gay, bi, trans and queer (LGBTQ) people were a mostly invisible minority. Very prejudicial and distorted
ideas of what they were like were held by many people. Those who
knew the truth--that LGBTQ people were pretty much like straight
people except for the added oppression they suffered because of their
sexuality--had the choice of remaining silent or becoming victims of
the prejudice themselves.

When LGBTQ people--the majority people of color--fought back
against police harassment in New York City in June 1969, it was a
signal to LGBTQ people everywhere that the time had come to challenge the historic legacy of oppression. This momentous event, the
Stonewall Rebellion, is commemorated every year by thousands of
LGBTQ people with marches and rallies in many cities.

LGBTQ people in large numbers continue fighting for an end to
the discrimination they face in all areas of their lives. LGBTQ people
are discriminated against by bosses and landlords. They face police

brutality and are physically attacked by bigots who know the cops and the courts will almost always side in their favor. The struggle continues for the right of LGBTQ people to marry--not because marriage is some "sacred institution," but to receive the hundreds of economic benefits given to married couples. LGBTQ youth are harassed at school and sometimes face homelessness after being kicked out of their homes.

LGBTQ people are also fighting erroneous ideas about them that are still widely held. For example, it is said that LGBTQ identity is rare, that it only exists in big cities, or in capitalist societies, or in families that are abnormal in one way or another. All these assertions are contradicted by facts that show that many people have homosexual feelings to one extent or another and that LGBTQ people have existed in all societies, at all times, whether persecuted or not and regardless of how a particular society was organized. (Through most of human existence the patriarchal family as we know it today did not exist.)

All progressive people should speak out for the rights of LGBTQ people. In addition, we should understand how the capitalists make use of the widespread prejudice against LGBTQ people to hurt all working and oppressed people. It is one more way to divide us, to keep us fighting among ourselves instead of uniting to defeat our common enemy, the capitalists who exploit LGBTQ and straight alike.

Self Determination

All workers, regardless of national background, have the same class interests. They all need to eliminate capitalist exploitation and replace the rule of the bosses with the rule of the workers--socialism.

It is clear that this tremendous task can't be achieved without the closest possible unity and trust among all workers. But when one or several sections of the working class are oppressed over and above the class as a whole, when in fact they belong to a people who constitute an oppressed nation, then the problems of unity are complicated.

Racism and national oppression are tools of the bosses. They divide the workers by making the more privileged group feel it is in their interest to go along with the terrible conditions imposed on the oppressed. The result is that all workers suffer, but the oppressed groups suffer by far the most.

The kind of solidarity that is needed to fight the bosses in the days ahead can only be built up through a struggle to break down the racism and inequality dividing the workers. The white workers must show by their actions that they will fight to extend to the oppressed people all the rights and benefits they already have.

But national oppression is not confined to the workplace. It is not expressed merely in lower wages and worse jobs. An oppressed nation is subject to humiliation, deprivation, scorn and repression in every area of social life. Therefore, much of their struggle is a political one to achieve democratic rights denied them.

Beginning with Karl Marx, communists or revolutionary socialists have always supported the right of oppressed nations to self-determination at the same time that they endeavored to unite the workers of all nationalities into a common fighting party of the working class.

Supporting the right of self-determination means supporting the oppressed people in whatever choice they may make about the type of political form that best suits their historical circumstances. This could be a federation of their national states with others; they might choose to form an autonomous region; they might feel that assimilation into the dominant nation with full equality can best serve their interests. Or they might want to establish a separate independent state of their own.

In the U.S. today, only the dominant white nation has a state of its own, and this is run by the billionaires. But the Black, Native, Latina/o and other oppressed nations don't have any type of state of their own, let alone a state run by the workers. They are systematically denied political power at all levels.

For white workers to understand the right of self-determination doesn't mean they should advocate separation, any more than it means that they should abandon the struggle to win over and change the view of backward whites who want to exclude Blacks and other oppressed peoples from their schools, neighborhoods, etc.

It is by supporting both the right of self-determination and the struggle for equality that white workers can help break down the racism that has divided our class and bring closer the day when all workers can cooperate in the struggle to tear down capitalist exploitation and oppression.

Culture

Dictionary.com defines culture as "the behaviors and beliefs characteristic of a particular social, ethnic, or age group." This definition is not necessarily incorrect, but it is wholly inadequate.

Culture is all encompassing. It is part of the superstructure. The thoughts, ideas, actions, language, arts—every human endeavor or expression is connected to a society's culture. It is not something static, but evolves and is intimately bound to the real and material world.

But where do these "behaviors and beliefs" come from?

The great revolutionary theorist from Guinea Bissau, Amilcar Cabral, wrote: "Culture, whatever the ideological or idealist characteristics of its expression, is ... an essential element of the history of a people. Culture is, perhaps, the resultant of this history just as the flower is the resultant of a plant. Like history, or because it is history, culture has as its material base the level of the productive forces and the mode of production."

Just as everything in nature goes through constant change, the thoughts and actions of human beings change to reflect the constantly changing world and how human beings interact with that reality.

Society is organized by that interaction--the manipulation of nature for subsistence. Karl Marx asserted, "By producing their means of subsistence men are indirectly producing their actual material life." Not every society developed at the same pace nor went through exactly the same stages in the same way, but how the needs of the society are met and the relation of the producers of the needs to the things produced is indeed what society is organized around. And, since it is from production that human nature is derived, it too is not a static thing.

When Marx said capital came into the world "dripping from head to toe from every pore with blood and dirt," he was speaking of the natural proclivity of the system. Private property, from which capitalism sprung, brought with it the subjugation of women, children, gender expression and sexual identity necessary for the patriarchal system to perpetuate the bequeathing of capital.

The particular history of building up the productive forces in the U.S.--that is to say, the history of slavery, genocide and theft of land--has left an indelible blemish on the conscience and consciousness of the society, and the people of the society.

U.S. capitalist society built its foundation off the super-exploitation of Africans who were brought as slaves; the stealing of land from Indigenous and Mexican people; and the genocide of Indigenous peoples. It was the belief of the supremacy of European or white people that led so many to accept the barbaric practice of accumulating capital.

How is it, then, that the people in the U.S. were able to elect the first Black president, Barack Obama, even though it does not represent full liberation for Black people? Especially when Black people are still vilified and nationally oppressed?

Forty years ago many whites did not want to swim in the same pool with Blacks and many didn't want their children to attend the same schools as Black children. There are many that still hold these racist views, but what changed to allow so many whites to see beyond race enough to elect a Black president?

It was struggle that changed the equation. When oppressed people and working people struggle against conditions imposed upon them, it affects consciousness as a whole. Old prejudices crumble and people become socialized to see past backward ways of thinking.

Here in the U.S., culture is often thought of as artistic output. While artistic output is only one aspect of culture, examining the arts--in this case music--is extremely useful to describe the peculiarities of U.S. society.

Jazz musician Miles Davis said of music: "Music is always changing. It changes because of the times and the technology that's available." Music is an important part of most people's lives. Everywhere you go there is music.

And, in the U.S. the music that is most pervasive is that of the oppressed. The music of Indigenous people, of the peoples of Latin America and especially of Black people and of the African Diaspora is predominant. It reflects the struggles of the people.

It too, though, is not free from the overarching culture of the capitalist system. While it speaks of the history of the oppressed, expressing their struggles and beliefs from earlier times, it suffers from the ideals that come with capitalist society, just as, in earlier times, it reflected the ideals that came with the modes of production, productive capabilities and social relations of those earlier societies.

Oppressed culture is always under attack and faces a great deal of scrutiny from capitalist media and the society as a whole. Hip-hop music is made the scapegoat for the sexism, racism and homophobia rampant in the U.S.

Whatever contradictions exist in rap music or any of the other elements of hip-hop, the culture is neither the greatest purveyor of the contradictions nor the initiator. It is merely subject to infiltration from the culture that comes with capitalist society.

Hip-hop began not just as party music, but as social commentary. What was then known as a counterculture—partly because hip-hop in its early days was underground—was a response to the conditions imposed upon Black and Puerto Rican youth in New York and across the country in inner-city areas in the late 1970s and 1980s. Those conditions included white flight from city areas, the beginning of deindustrialization and the decline of the great social movements of the 1960s and 1970s as a result of the boom-and-bust cycle of capitalism.

If the perpetuation of capital requires greater and greater exploitation, especially of oppressed nationalities, then it is natural for countercultures of the exploited—the oppressed and workers—in bourgeois or capitalist society to exist. The wellspring, in this period, of the countercultures shows the desire for freedom from exploitation.

The artistic expression of pop or mass culture can be a gauge of the willingness of the masses to struggle, expressions of the conditions the masses are faced with, or both at the same time. The same goes for the culture of the oppressed—those workers who face added discrimination, repression and hardship because of race, ethnicity, gender, sexuality, so-called legal status and/or disability.

However, the culture of the oppressed not only faces infiltration from the ideals of the ruling class, but also from the dominant layer of society. In the U.S. that layer is white. Because of the history of genocide, land theft and slavery—part of "the primitive accumulation of capital" denoted by Marx—race is always a factor. The historical development of the U.S. and the world has deemed that the lens of race is always firmly fitted.

When capitalism is abolished from the Earth, new ideas and beliefs will come and human nature will evolve to reflect the changed social relations and the changing material life.

How the State Arose

When Marxists speak of the state it is not in the sense that many in the U.S. are accustomed to; it is not in reference to, for instance, the state of New York, Ohio or California. What is meant is the repressive apparatus of the government.

Some may even confuse the government with the state, but the state is wielded by the government—which is part of the superstructure of capitalist or bourgeois society.

The superstructure of capitalist society is born of the objective conditions of a society, based on profit derived from exploitation and from the social relations of such society.

The state, simply, as the repressive apparatus of the government—the courts, the prisons, the police, and the military—stands to maintain the social relations as they are, to protect the owning and possessing few from the exploited and oppressed masses.

Has the state always existed? This question can partly be answered by posing another: Have there always been classes?

Examining history through the science of materialism is required to see the basis for the need of the state.

Human beings have existed on the Earth for hundreds of thousands of years, but the organization of human societies under the rule of the state is only maybe 6,000 years or so.

If one were to measure history by a yardstick, then the period of history where the state has existed would account for less than an inch.

For hundreds of thousands of years human beings lived in societies that had no state—no cops, no jails, no armies.

Disputes were handled through social mediation and pressure.

What conditions then produced the state? How did the state arise from the older stateless societies?

The state first came into existence around 4,000 B.C. Before that, societies existed communally, sharing as necessary because of scarcity. As production capability began to change, a surplus beyond what was necessary to survive from one day to the next was produced.

The surplus was hoarded and made the private property of a few, while the majority had no property. From this came the split of humanity into classes: the propertied, and those who possessed no property.

An apparatus, the state, grew from antagonisms between the propertied and the non-propertied. The state existed then, in its earlier forms, as it does now--as specially trained and armed people who protect the interests of the few owners of wealth from the great majority who are impoverished.

It is from these early conditions that ancient slave society emerged, where human beings became property of the wealthy.

The Roman Empire was a slave society. More than 50 percent of the society was enslaved. To maintain this reality, the Romans needed a vast army of thousands of soldiers whose primary tasks were to protect the status quo, put down slave rebellions and conquer more territory.

While the Roman Empire collapsed, it was eventually replaced by another form of the state. In the feudal state, serfs toiled on land owned by feudal lords. Wealth was derived from serfs paying the great majority of what they produced to the feudal lords, keeping only a meager portion with which they could barely sustain themselves and their families. The armies of feudal society were kept and paid by the lords, who used them to suppress the serfs.

The capitalist class arose in opposition to the landed aristocracy. This early capitalist class was composed of merchants and shopkeepers eager to produce more wealth through commerce and trade. In bloody civil wars, in one country after the other, they overthrew the old ruling powers to set up a state to serve their needs where the old state formation could not.

The capitalist states that arose in Europe and later in the U.S. used vast armies to subdue the people of Asia, Africa and the Americas in order to exploit them and their natural resources. Most people around the world had lived in societies with earlier formations of the state or where there existed no state at all, such as many of the peoples of North America and the Caribbean.

The imperialist nations of Europe and the U.S. have developed the state to huge proportions, building vast armies with enormous budgets and high-tech weaponry that can destroy whole cities.

The state and its reason for existence is more apparent as more and more oppressed and exploited people in the U.S. and around the world fight back against the conditions imposed upon them.

The State Today

The previous chapter traced the evolution of the state--the army, courts, cops, prisons and tax collectors--from its formation 6,000 years ago. This state has consistently served the privileged classes-- first slave owners, then feudal lords and, today, the capitalists.

The U.S. has developed one of the most extensive and brutal states in human history. This state appropriates the meager earnings of the working class to finance its huge armies of war and occupation, which it deploys at will to countries such as Iraq and Afghanistan; and to fund the police state and prison system, which presently imprisons well over two million people, half of whom are people of color.

Hundreds of billions more are spent on the courts that administer this injustice, as well as domestic and international surveillance activities operated through the FBI and the CIA.

This vast apparatus is necessary to serve and protect the power of the minority of billionaires who rule this country from the corporate boardrooms to the halls of Congress. The character of the state as a tool of the bosses is reaffirmed every time striking workers are jailed by the courts; it is reaffirmed every time a young unarmed Black man dies at the hands of a racist police officer. Every time a country is "shocked and awed" into submission, this character is displayed for the world to see.

The state has become almost completely merged with the capitalist class itself, creating a virtual shuttle service from boardrooms to government office, and providing a conduit of limitless funds from the government coffers to the bank accounts of finance and industry executives. How else can you explain the connections between former President George W. Bush and Vice President Dick Cheney to the oil and energy industry? Why else would President Barack Obama name Timothy Geithner as Treasury Secretary and have him funnel trillions of dollars to the banks on Wall Street in the name of fiscal stimulus?

The ruthlessness of the capitalist state has been revealed many times in recent years--in Iraq and Afghanistan, where imperialist bombs and gunfire have killed countless children; in New Orleans and the Mississippi Delta, where the Black survivors of Hurricane Katrina faced an assault on their livelihoods by the same government that failed to protect them from the disaster; and in Oakland, Calif., where Oscar Grant, an unarmed young Black man, was shot dead by police as he lay handcuffed and face down on the platform of a train station.

The Bolshevik Revolution of 1917 demonstrated the capacity for the existence of a new kind of state--a workers' state. This revolution abolished capitalism in Russia, just as slavery and serfdom had been overthrown before. All wealth, except personal property, was made the common property of all workers. The economy was planned to meet human needs, not the profits of the few.

The Soviet state existed in the historic interests of the entire world's working class and oppressed. Despite its deficiencies, and its eventual defeat in 1991, the Soviet state was an inspiration for socialist revolutions in China, Cuba, Vietnam and other countries around the globe. Even today, after many of these countries have experienced counter-revolutions or have turned toward the market, millions around the world are fighting and dying for the establishment of a new state of this kind. Workers and the poor in countries as varied as Colombia,

Venezuela, Nepal, India, and the Philippines struggle daily for a workers' state like the one Cubans have been building for 50 years. As the economic crisis in the U.S. escalates more and more, workers at home will start to demand a new state as well.

The state has always been an instrument of dictatorship: of the slave owner over the slave, the feudal lord over the serf, the capitalist over the workers and oppressed. The workers' state maximizes democracy for the working class as it exercises a dictatorship over the remnants of the former capitalist ruling class.

The growth of socialism holds the promise of abolishing all class antagonisms. The overthrow of capitalism worldwide will set the stage for the gradual disappearance of the state as the world currently knows it. It will provide the conditions for the world's wealth, produced in abundance by modern technology, to be shared in common. Capitalism's demise will unlock the potential for humans to live in a modern, peaceful society, without any need for the old state's instruments of suppression.

Democracy

The word "democracy" is Greek in origin. Literally it means "rule of the people." In a democracy, the control of society is supposed to be held not by the elite, but by everyone, equally. Democracy is often held up as the opposite of a dictatorship, in which a small group has the power.

The U.S. government portrays itself as a shining example of democracy. Children are taught from their first days of school that the U.S. has a democratic government "of the people, by the people, and for the people."

Formal elections are held up as proof of this democracy. Every few years voters can go to the polls and vote for a candidate for president, Congress, governor, the state legislature, mayor, city council and so on. This, the ruling class tells us, is democracy.

But how democratic is the U.S. really? Every candidate who wishes to have a chance of winning a major election needs a great deal of money. The majority of this money comes from Wall Street banks like

Goldman Sachs, Citigroup and National City. The media, which has a disproportionate influence on the decisions of voters, is privately owned by wealthy corporations as well.

The majority of people in this society are members of the working class, yet only a tiny minority of the politicians are ever workers, especially workers of color. Most major politicians come from the ruling class or are hired agents for that class. Both President George W. Bush and Vice President Dick Cheney were themselves wealthy capitalists, as are many members of Congress.

Occasionally, because of historic circumstance, someone who is neither a member of the ruling class nor one of its direct hired agents can win a big election. The 2008 election of President Barack Obama, the first election of a Black president, is an example of this exception to the rule. Even when this happens the capitalist institutions of government act as a brake on democracy and prevent the implementation of real reform. This can be seen by the compromises Obama has had to make in order to secure and keep the presidency, such as his nominations of Hillary Clinton for Secretary of State, Timothy Geithner for Secretary of the Treasury, and his retention of Robert Gates for Secretary of Defense.

The U.S. economy is not operated in a democratic fashion. The workers and oppressed live under a dictatorship of the capitalists. If the owner of a factory wants to make machine guns instead of medical equipment, the workers at the plant have no recognized right to challenge that decision. If that same factory owner decides to close the plant down and lay off everybody, no one can legally stop the owner.

Workers spend forty hours or more a week under the dictatorship of the bosses, if they are lucky enough to have a job. The rest of the time the workers purchase the bosses' electricity, eat the food the bosses make money on, sleep in the houses the banks own, and pay interest to the banks on credit cards.

This situation makes it impossible for the capitalist government to operate above the class situation on the ground. Even if the politicians aren't tied directly to the capitalist class, it is impossible for them not to be pressured by the tremendous power and wealth of the bosses. The state and the government do not stand above society--they were set up in the beginning to protect the interests of the ruling class.

Capitalist governments operate in the same way that capitalist economies run--as a dictatorship of the capitalist ruling class. Capitalist democracy acts as a democracy for the rich and as a dictatorship against the workers and oppressed. The institutions of government and the procedures for elections are intended to allow capitalists to settle disputes among themselves. They do not empower workers with the democracy they need in their economic and political lives.

Workers have been able to win some rights from the capitalist dictatorship, but these rights were won as concessions to workers' struggle. Continual struggle is necessary to prevent the capitalist dictatorship from rescinding the rights and freedoms won. Despite the insistence of politicians that elections represent real democracy, it's clear who really runs the show. The dictatorship of the capitalists can be seen in the trillions of dollars in handouts Presidents Bush and Obama have given to the banks in the midst of the worst economic crisis for workers since the Great Depression. The continuation of troops in Iraq and the escalation of war in Afghanistan also demonstrate the limited impact elections can have under capitalist democracy.

The U.S. is about as democratic in its conduct internationally as it is at home. When the U.S. invades nations, it insists that it is "spreading democracy." But the U.S. government has propped up brutal dictatorships all around the world when the interests of the ruling class of bankers and capitalists were threatened by a people's movement.

In Chile, when the people democratically elected Socialist Salvador Allende as president in the 1970s, the U.S. sent in the CIA to overthrow him and then installed General Pinochet, a brutal dictator who massacred thousands of innocent people and suspended all civil liberties.

All across the world, the "democracy" the U.S. champions has been revealed as a cover for profit and exploitation. If a leader serves the interests of U.S. bankers and capitalists, he is supported by the U.S. government. If a leader opposes them, he is often labeled a "dictator" who must be "removed" in the capitalist government and the press.

Real democracy would mean the working class majority rules. Real democracy would mean democratic control of the factories, mines, offices and farms, with directors elected by the workers, from among the workers. The government would be an extension of this workers' control. It would coordinate and plan production to meet people's needs and prevent the capitalists from retaking power. The type and amount of items produced would be determined by societal needs and not by the profit motive.

Such a democracy can only exist after the capitalist ruling class is destroyed. Then real democracy, the democracy of the workers, would exercise a dictatorship over the remnants of the former capitalist ruling class until such a time that classes have withered away along with the police, courts and jails that protect them.

Reformism

Throughout the history of capitalism, the workers have had leaders who have guided the struggles that won the few basic rights we have today: the eight-hour work day, the right to unionize, and an end to child labor are just a few examples.

We can generally divide the leaders who have fought for these things into two main groups: reformists and revolutionaries.

A reformist tries to improve and reform the living conditions for the workers within the capitalist system (tries to make the system more "humane"), while the revolutionary fights for the same reforms as part of the larger struggle to smash capitalism. It is this fear of outright revolution that has forced the ruling class and the state into making concessions to the legitimate demands of workers.

The reformists often sincerely sympathize with the workers, but they do not understand the real cause of the exploitation and misery of the working class. They generally believe that the crimes of capitalism are just a tragic misunderstanding, and if only the bosses could be made to realize the suffering they are causing, things could be better. Some believe that oppression comes just because the capitalists are greedy, and take the burden off the system of capitalism. A reformist struggle is like putting a band-aid on a bullet wound.

Reformists take the capitalist system for granted, believing that the system can be made more human but that changing to a better system is impossible. Because of this outlook they are forced to limit their demands to ones that don't challenge the bosses' rule.

"Of course you need a raise, but if you ask for too much, how is the company going to stay in business?" How many times have the workers been force-fed this line as an excuse for making concessions to the boss?

Ralph Nader is a typical reformist. After exposing in detail the criminal practices of the automotive and other industries, he proposed a mild legislative program to break up the monopolies and bring back a mythical age of small capitalism and fair competition that never existed. There are two reasons legislative reforms similar to Nader's proposals are unworkable. First, capitalism naturally tends towards monopoly and monopolies have dominated the system since before World War I. Second, the monopolies have also dominated the politicians and now dominate them more than ever.

Revolutionaries are the most militant fighters for improvements in the standard of living and for defending the rights of workers, the poor, and the oppressed under capitalism.

Revolutionaries strive to lead the struggle in the trade unions, tenant groups, consumer groups, organizations of welfare recipients and unemployed workers, groups fighting higher food prices or housing foreclosures.

While reformists are not the class enemy and often win supporters because of their legitimate struggle with the bosses, they are unable to consciously lead a struggle against capitalism because they themselves believe in it. By not showing the workers who their real enemy is, the reformist way of thinking helps capitalism to continue and to oppress the workers even more effectively.

But revolutionaries lead these struggles with a view to enlarging them, deepening them, and with the aim of getting into a still greater struggle to overthrow the whole rotten, oppressive system.

The Labor
Bureaucracy

Sometimes union leaders get paid as much as a boss. They wheel and deal with the politicians in the back rooms like a boss. When it comes time to call a strike or fight hard for a better contract, sometimes you think they are listening to the boss.

But are the labor bureaucrats really the same as the bosses?

The bureaucrats depend on the existence of the unions for their jobs, and so are forced to fight the bosses enough to keep unions intact. In fact, in order for the antagonisms of class society to be maintained, the existence of a labor bureaucracy is necessary.

Bureaucrats are caught between the workers and the bosses. On the one hand, they want to keep the workers quiet; because the more organized the workers are against the bosses, the more they have the power to take away the bureaucrats' privileges. On the other hand, the bureaucrats cannot work completely for the bosses, because the bosses are generally opposed to the very existence of unions. Even buying the bureaucrats off costs the bosses money. The bosses' struggle against the unions, however, is as much about maintaining power as it is about immediate profit margins.

The bureaucrats often take the bosses' side. They may hold the union back, stop it from organizing new workers and encourage workers to participate in less threatening political action. Much of the top leadership of the traditional AFL-CIO and Change to Win unions are unwilling to engage in a serious fight against the bosses. These leaders are often guilty of backroom deals with the boss that cut the workers out of the process and sell working class interests short.

Real rank-and-file leadership is still visible in some independent unions and at the local level of some of the traditional unions. The United Electrical, Radio and Machine Workers, International Longshore Workers Local 10, United Steelworkers Local 8751 (Boston School Bus Drivers), and many others around the country offer a glimpse of what the labor movement could achieve if rank-and-file workers were empowered.

The bureaucrats often support the bosses' imperialist wars. For the labor movement, there is a real danger of drawing national chauvinistic and protectionist conclusions from objective developments that divert the struggle away from the companies. The labor bureaucrats do nothing to avoid this crisis; in fact, they usually fall prey to it by building campaigns around "American Made" products and providing misleading information to workers about the benefits of supporting the anti-worker, pro-war Democratic Party. Many resources are diverted from the organizing of workers into unions and put into canvassing campaigns to support Democratic Party candidates.

How did these class-collaborationist labor bureaucrats get control of the unions, which were born out of the bitter struggles of workers for their basic rights?

The main reason they were able to gain control was by winning support from the more privileged and skilled workers, who do not typically suffer from national or special oppressions. The bureaucrats, most of whom came from this more privileged section of the working class--what we call the labor aristocracy--have been bought off by the extra money and privileges that the ruling class had to offer as a result of the super-profits they had made from imperialism. They used the unions to defend these privileges before anything else. So, indirectly, the ruling class was able to buy off a part of the workers.

Still, without the unions the bureaucrats are nothing. With the growing economic crisis, the pressure is on them to act. And if they want to keep their jobs, they're going to have to fight the bosses. Because if they can't keep up with the struggle of the rank and file, they are going to be waiting on the unemployment lines like everybody else!

Fascism

Nowadays when people speak of fascism, they speak of Nazis and jack boots, Mussolini, and Franco.

Classical fascism gained a mass base among the ruined middle classes in Europe after the First World War, when economic crisis, especially in Germany and Italy, drove millions to look for a strong leader. In Germany, an attempt to carry out a workers' revolution in 1918 had failed. Fascist demagogues, using anti-capitalist rhetoric, deflected mass anger into extreme nationalism and the scapegoating of minorities. They violently broke up workers' organizations, attacking communists and socialists. Eventually the fascists got the support from big capital that they needed to take over the capitalist state, laying the basis for a second imperialist world war.

Fascism is an extreme right-wing form of capitalist rule. Fascist ideologies still exist in different forms in most capitalist countries and in former colonies that are ruled by puppet regimes. In the U.S. fascism is closely linked to the ideology of white supremacy and shows itself in many institutions and cultural tendencies.

Fascism celebrates the nation, the race, or the state as a community transcending all other loyalties. It emphasizes a myth of national re-birth after what it calls a period of decline (read from today's pundits: "a return to American values"). Fascism celebrates unity and power through military strength. It can promote a sense of superiority, im-perialist expansion and genocide against communities of color.

State-sanctioned violence against groups who hold opposing po-litical views is also a manifestation of fascism--thus Hitler's Germany targeted Communists as well as Jews. Fascism is a last resort of the ruling class, which uses it to smash all working-class organizations. In a pure fascist society, working class political parties and trade unions are outlawed, social legislation is overturned, civil liberties are re-scinded, and democratic institutions are destroyed or subverted, all in order to keep the capitalists in power.

While those characteristics fulfill the technical definition of fas-cism, the meaning of words can change over time along with the ex-periences of people. Therefore, today in the U.S., many Black, Asian, and Latina/o workers, Native peoples, immigrant workers, LGBTQ people, youth, and students feel that the capitalist state policies they struggle against represent fascism.

Some Marxists contend that people of color in the U.S. have always lived under a form of semi-fascism. U.S. policies responsible for the genocide of Native peoples; the enslavement of African people; the theft of half of Mexico and the resulting oppression of the Chicana/o people of the Southwest; the theft of Hawaii and Puerto Rico; the rise of the prison-industrial complex; the passage of the Patriot Act; do-mestic wiretapping and spying on political organizations; and other forms of severe state repression, either historic or current, have been likened to fascism by the impacted communities.

Fascism's approach to politics is both populist--in that it seeks to activate "the people" as a whole against perceived oppressors or en-emies--and elitist--in that it treats the people's will as embodied in one leader, supported by big business interests, and from whom au-thority proceeds downward. Fascist tendencies can become stronger during periods of economic downturn, when middle class elements as well as workers are hurting and more likely to buy in to demagogu-ery against immigrants, LGBTQ people and workers of color and place their hope in the false promises of renewal that fascism claims to bring. Workers, particularly white workers, have a responsibility to resist the capitalist policies some view as fascist and to fight back against the potential resurgence of traditional fascist movements during times of economic crisis.

Revolution

The Bolshevik Revolution in 1917 smashed the Russian capitalist state and brought a workers' party to power for the first time in history. Later revolutions in China, Vietnam, Korea, Cuba and elsewhere would smash the existing state in those countries and bring parties of workers and peasants to power. In each case the workers' party, or communist party, was dedicated to the construction of socialism and the long-term transition to a fully communist society.

Workers and students often question exactly what constitutes a revolution and what does not. The media often confuses the issue further by referring to any big change as a revolution, like the so-called Republican Revolution of 1994.

A revolution is much more than a big event, however radical or life-changing that event may be. A genuine social revolution is represented by the overthrow of one class by another. This overthrow occurs when the contradictions and conflict inherent in existing social and economic relations become an intolerable burden on society's development. The revolution itself sets free new advanced social relations and marks the beginning of a whole new economic system.

A genuine revolution is necessarily violent. The present revolutionary class of workers and oppressed would obviously prefer to have a peaceful revolution in which their friends and loved ones were not the target of violence by the state. History, however, has clearly demonstrated that no ruling class has ever given up its power without a violent fight. Existing class rule is based on the organized violence of the police and army. Workers and their allies must be prepared to defend themselves by any means necessary in the course of a revolutionary struggle.

All changes of class rule in recorded history have come about by revolution. The Glorious Revolution in England and the French Revolution represented the process by which the capitalist class came to power in these two countries and smashed the old feudal state and feudal social relations. These revolutions laid the political basis for the rapid development of industry and technology. The capitalist class was the revolutionary class at this time in its struggle against the vestiges of feudal power.

Today the capitalist class is the reactionary class that holds back the productive potential of workers as it oppresses them. The workers of the world make up the revolutionary class with the historic potential for the overthrow of the bourgeoisie. Not all revolutionary struggles are successful; and the international revolution has suffered severe setbacks following the defeat of the socialist-bloc countries of the Soviet Union and Eastern Europe. Despite these temporary and serious setbacks, the working class has not ceded its historic mission of socialist revolution.

The counterrevolutions in the former socialist-bloc countries illustrate the need to continually struggle against the retrograde trends of bureaucratism and privilege which separate the communist party and workers' state from its natural base in the working class. These trends developed over time in the socialist-bloc countries and preceded the eventual defeat of the revolution by domestic reaction allied with imperialism.

Mao Zedong, the founding chairperson of the Communist Party of China, foresaw this possibility in China and sought to head it off by launching the Great Proletarian Cultural Revolution in 1966.

The Cultural Revolution was a recognition of the need for continual revolution in all spheres of society--political, economic and cultural. The theory of continual revolution explicitly acknowledges that the process of socialist revolution within a particular country does not end at the exact moment workers smash the old state and establish a revolutionary state in its place.

Socialist revolution represents the conquering of state power by the exploited masses for the first time in history. All previous revolutions have transferred power from one small ruling class of exploiters to another class of exploiters. Modern technology lays the basis for material abundance and provides the opportunity for the producers of wealth to run society.

The working class cannot rely on the old state mechanisms developed to serve capitalism in its revolutionary struggle. Elections, for example, may be a barometer of how the masses feel, but they cannot in and of themselves bring workers to power. Workers must create their own instruments of power to carry through the revolution.

The working class needs a party which understands its role in history and is organized under the centralized leadership of workers and the oppressed to assist in the development of these instruments of power. This party must come from and be embedded in the exploited masses so that it can move decisively when a revolutionary situation presents itself. Only through the leadership of such a communist party can the working class smash the old capitalist state and replace it with a revolutionary dictatorship based on workers' power. The final victory of workers' revolution throughout the entire world will definitively end the basis for all exploitation.

Socialism

Socialism is a system in which the working class controls the means of production and the distribution and exchange of goods. A socialist society is a society ruled not by the elite, but by the masses of people.

Socialism takes the ownership of the means of production away from the capitalist class and places it in the hands of the working class, or society as a whole. The factories, the giant farms, the banking system, the media, transportation, health care, communications, and education are no longer run on the basis of advancing profits. Instead, they are run on the basis of fulfilling human needs. Instead of unaccountable CEOs and capitalists having control of these "commanding heights" of the economy, the people will maintain control through democratic bodies.

Socialism organizes the means of production according to a plan based on utilizing the available resources to meet the needs of society. This plan unfetters the productive potential of labor, allowing the state to provide basic necessities at no cost to the individual. Socialism is thus able to provide health care, education, food, housing and recreation to every person.

Increasing production under socialism means more shared wealth for all. Under capitalism, however, increased production leads to crises. Production periodically outstrips consumption because workers' wages are under constant downward pressure from the bosses, who must continually raise productivity and shed workers in order to compete and make profit. The result is overproduction, such as in the housing market, where millions of homes stand vacant because the banks and developers can't sell them at a profit. At the same time, millions of families are in crisis for lack of decent, affordable housing.

Socialism allows for the elimination of unemployment, since a reserve army of labor is no longer needed to intensify competition among workers and drive wages down. Technology will no longer be used as a pretext to lay off workers and increase exploitation, but will be used to free workers from monotonous and dangerous work. As the need for production workers decreases with new technology, a socialist society can provide more employment and training in areas of human development like health, education, culture and recreation, as well as science and technology to benefit people and the environment. Without capitalist crises, there will be no drastic budget cuts in these areas but instead dynamic growth.

Socialism allows the working class, the new rulers of society, to begin to beat down the old forces of oppression. Racism, sexism, homophobia, and all other discriminatory ideologies used by the ruling class to justify economic, political, social and cultural inequality will be eliminated as society progresses down the road of socialism.

Socialist Countries

Socialism, a system in which the working class takes control of the means of production and the distribution and exchange of goods, is not just a fantasy, pipe dream, utopian vision, or good idea. In fact, even though socialism was generally constructed despite a history of underdevelopment and imperialist intervention, this new economic system has proven itself to be far superior to capitalism.

Prior to the 1917 Bolshevik Revolution, for example, Russia and the surrounding countries which eventually made up the Soviet Union were impoverished. Famine and starvation were common. Women were exploited in the virtual captivity of their homes as well as in the factories and fields. Workers labored long hours for very little pay. Peasants worked all summer growing and harvesting crops, only to be forced to turn them over to the land-owning nobility at the end of the season, leaving them barely enough to survive the winter. Education was unheard of for the vast majority of the population, and illiteracy was rampant.

But the Bolshevik Revolution of 1917 laid the foundation for the formation of the Soviet Union and efforts to construct socialism. A new government, led by the Communist Party and drawing power from councils of workers, peasants and soldiers, was established. The workplace was democratized.

This new workers' state became an inspiration to the workers and oppressed all around the world. Within a short period of time the Soviet Union was able to industrialize a backward country, get rid of landlords and collectivize agriculture, and provide free and universal health care and education to all. No one can forget, of course, the Soviet Union's most significant contribution to humanity--the military defeat of the invading armies of Nazi Germany during World War II. This war against fascism cost the Soviet Union tens of millions of lives and destroyed much of its industry. The victory over fascism was followed by the Cold War, which further weakened the Soviet bloc.

Workers in China, Korea, Vietnam, Cuba, Eastern Europe and other parts of the world were inspired by socialism's ability to build up the forces of production. Over time the ruling classes were overturned in these countries and revolutionary governments were established that adopted socialist programs to meet the material needs of the masses.

The international working class was dealt a major setback with the defeat of the socialist-bloc countries of Eastern Europe and the Soviet Union from 1989-1991. Workers in the former socialist bloc countries were extremely affected, as infant mortality increased precipitously, the quality of education and health care was drastically reduced, and social ills such as drug abuse were reintroduced into society for the first time in decades.

However, the counterrevolutions that swept the Soviet Union and Eastern Europe, while they affected other socialist countries, did not necessarily bring them down.

Socialist Cuba has managed to survive horrendous attacks from the U.S. Only 90 miles south of the Florida coast of the U.S., Cuba has the highest life expectancy in Latin America and the Caribbean, as well as the highest literacy rate. Cuba's infant mortality rate is lower than that of the U.S. Cuba sends more medical aid abroad than any country on earth. Cuba even provides medical training for people around the world, where they can come and be taught medicine for free on the condition that they use their knowledge to provide care in their home communities to people who have not able to obtain it.

The Democratic People's Republic of Korea also stands tall as an example of a country that has resisted imperialist aggression and instituted socialist measures. The DPRK has provided universal education, housing, health care and literacy for its population. It has stood up to intense U.S. interference and the threat of invasion by tens of thousands of U.S. troops right on its border.

Communist parties still retain their monopoly on power in China and Vietnam following the revolutions in those two countries. Decades of risky market experimentation, however, have allowed the growth of a capitalist class and placed China's socialist system in a precarious position. At the same time, the working class in China has also grown enormously, along with the development of the means of production. U.S. imperialism tries to undermine the Chinese Communist Party because it is the main organized political force in China that protects the remaining elements of that country's socialist system. A full counterrevolution in China and the removal of the CPC from power would have devastating consequences for the well-being of China's one-billion-plus workers and farmers.

The corporate media, which is owned by the very people Marxists seek to overthrow, would like workers to believe that the defeat of socialism in the Soviet Union and Eastern Europe represents a failure of Marxism. A closer analysis of history, however, demonstrates that it was the intense economic, political and military pressures on these countries from imperialism that made them vulnerable. While the world revolution has experienced a temporary setback, the advances made by countries engaged in building socialism remain a source of inspiration to the worldwide working class and the oppressed nations.

Communism

The latest scientific view is that human beings first evolved from earlier primates more than 200,000 years ago in Africa. Since then we have spread over the whole world. The state first appeared in a few places on the globe about 6,000 years ago. Before that, and continuing in many parts of the world up until recent times, there was a very long period of human development known to Marxists as primitive communism, where people existed without private property or the governments and laws that protect propertied classes. They lived in small groups and shared what little they had. This period is described as primitive because modern technology and science did not exist, and communist because there were no economic classes.

As techniques improved, the eventual accumulation of surpluses lent itself to the development of classes. The development of classes lent itself to class conflict. The privileged classes sought to secure their rule permanently and developed state-like structures with laws protecting the ownership of property and armed organizations to enforce those laws. In today's world of multi-billionaires and paupers, where there are huge standing armies and police agencies, the state has grown to grotesque proportions.

Once this parasitic and outmoded ruling class has been defeated, the technology available even now will have laid the basis for society to start transitioning through the stages of socialism until it reaches a modern form of communism, based on abundance instead of scarcity. The science of Marxism predicts that as the capitalist states are permanently defeated worldwide and revolutionary workers' states replace them and take up the task of building socialism, the very existence of the state will become unnecessary and the state will start to wither away.

At this point human beings will live in a stateless society without classes, but with the advantages of modern science and technology. This is communism, the final goal of Marxist-Leninists. Communists fight for a world without poverty, racism, sexism, homophobia, or exploitation of any kind. Revolutionaries will continue to press harder and harder until this final goal is achieved and a world without oppression is the order of the day.

F.I.S.T. Program

1. The Right to Free Public Education and Job Training with Stipend

We believe that education at all levels is a right and that this includes training in all vocational fields. Young people should be free to determine their career without fear of drowning in debt incurred by rising tuition fees.

We believe that the great expenditure on war, jails and prisons and on corporate welfare is a crime; and that these billions could instead partly be used towards providing education for all and guaranteeing jobs.

Education is a lifelong endeavor, not only to provide a person the tools to be productive in society, but also to connect a person and their surroundings to events in history. We therefore believe that the long view of history and the science of human and societal development should be taught.

The history of all oppressed nationalities and the true history of colonization of their lands and subjugation of their people should be taught as well, rather than the oppressors slant on history that is taught in schools across the country. To this end, we support all oppressed people and their right to educate their own people

2. The Demilitarization of Our Schools

Today many schools, especially those in inner cities and neighborhoods of oppressed nationalities, look like prisons: bars on the windows, metal detectors at entrances and roving police patrols. These things are not conducive to a positive learning environment and serve to intimidate and criminalize young people.

Military recruiters should not be allowed access to young people. With college tuition increasing and access to loans decreasing, the military option appears more attractive to youth uncertain about their economic future and that of their families. Recruiters spread lies to persuade youth to join a military that is used to wage war in the interests of a system that perpetuates exploitation.

As a whole the No Child Left Behind Act should be repealed, and especially the portion that allows recruiters access to students.

3. The Right to Healthcare

Millions of poor and working people lack access to medical care, and the greatest disparity can be seen amongst oppressed nationalities. The resources wasted by the military and the Pentagon for the aims of the rich and super rich could be used to provide a national healthcare system for every person in the U.S.

There should be a government healthcare program providing 100% coverage for all people, including vision, dental, and reproductive health.

Such a thing would make insurance companies completely obsolete. In fact, health insurance companies view healthcare as a commodity and that is what it has become, instead of a form of subsistence for oppressed and workers. As a right, it frees workers to be healthy, productive members of society

4. The Right to Housing

Housing, as all things necessary to live a healthy life and maintain dignity, is a right. Why should people be thrown out or evicted from their residence because of inability to pay? Why should there be millions of homeless people, many of them with families in tow when there is no shortage of housing?

Housing prices have become astronomical and in many cases account for 50% or more of a person's income. Millions of homes and apartments sit empty when there are people that could use them. This is a crime.

What's more, landlords have become increasingly restrictive in who they rent to, denying people based on credit scores or criminal records.

There needs to be guaranteed housing. A massive works program may not even be necessary, except to repair and make livable crumbling apartment buildings and public housing. In many cases, the government can simply seize empty homes and apartments and move people into them.

And, seeing as the government owns 75% of the country's mortgages after having taken over Fannie Mae and Freddie Mac, an indefinite moratorium should be issued and terms favorable to workers and the poor can be determined.

5. Stop the Raids and Deportations

It is an undeniable truth that the people of Latin America, who make up the largest percentage of immigrant workers, are the original inhabitants of the Americas. So to label any Latin American as an "illegal alien" is to wipe away thousands of years of history.

We believe that no human being is "illegal" except the imperialists and that as capital is free to flow--interrupting the livelihoods of people across the globe--people should be free to travel, especially to escape conditions imposed upon them by the ravages of imperialist intervention in their homelands.

We believe that all workers, be they from the Caribbean, Latin America, Africa, Asia or Europe are driven to the U.S. ultimately because of imperialism.

We demand that the government cease all raids and deportations, which interrupt lives including the lives of young people, many of whom were born in the U.S. and are being separated from their families.

Immigrant workers should not be the scapegoats of the rich who want to drive down wages for all the oppressed and workers. This scapegoating is racist in nature and meant to pit U.S.-born oppressed and workers from foreign-born oppressed and workers.

6. The Right to a Job or an Income

The oppressed and workers have a right to employment. Many young people have dropped out of the job market altogether, because of the dim prospects of securing a gainful, well paying job.

A large swath of territory was devastated by the deindustrialization period in the U.S. This did not have to happen. Oppressed people and workers should not have to pay for the greed and mismanagement of corporations. Those who work should be able to determine the fate of their jobs.

There is much that could be done in the U.S. A program of much-needed improvements in infrastructure, especially in the inner city, would provide for hundreds of thousands of jobs. Young people could take pride in being productive members of society, instead of the dread that they face because of an uncertain future.

7. The Right to a Clean and Healthy Enviornment

Workers have the right to breathe clean air, drink safe water, and consume healthy, untainted foods. Capitalism has threatened this right through profit-driven industrial pollution and the damaging effects of imperialist wars of conquest. Young workers and students are particularly impacted by environmental degradation as the true effects of today's pollution will be felt decades from now.

We demand an end to the environmental racism exemplified by selective enforcement of environmental rules and regulations in communities of color, the intentional targeting of these communities for placement of polluting industries, and the exclusion of these community leaders from regulatory bodies.

We demand worker and community control of industry for the creation of a sustainable ecology in contrast to the anarchy of capitalist production.

8. Shut down the prison industrial complex

As job opportunities, student loans and options in general for youth steadily disappear, youth are increasingly being railroaded into the prison industrial complex. In fact, prisons and the military seem to be the most viable option for many youth in urban cities. Especially affected by the criminal injustice system are youth of color; lesbian, gay, bi and trans youth; and immigrant youth.

Rather than reverse this trend--by funding education, jobs programs, extracurricular activities and social services--federal, state and local governments can be seen pouring money into more law enforcement and more jails.

We demand an end to the criminalization of youth for the way they dress and talk; to the quelling of righteous dissent amongst youth and students; to police brutality on the streets and a racist and unjust court system. We further demand an end to the racist death penalty, and freedom for all political prisoners, including Mumia Abu-Jamal, Leonard Peltier and so many others who have been imprisoned simply for defending the rights of themselves and their communities.

9. Self-determination is a right

In the face of hundreds of years, since the very founding of the United States, of outright oppression and repression of communities of color throughout the U.S.--slavery, the theft of Native lands including more than half of Mexico, the enforced sterilization of women of color, lynchings, concentration camps for Japanese Americans, the wholesale incarceration of people of color, and on and on--we demand the right of oppressed communities to determine their own destiny.

We affirm the right of oppressed communities to decide what is best for their own communities, and the right for them to fight for those rights by any means necessary. We support any demands for reparations, in whatever form, that oppressed communities may make upon the racist U.S. government.

10. Defeat U.S. imperialism

As we make demands for self-determination within oppressed communities in the U.S., we also affirm these rights for oppressed nations around the world, many of which are fighting valiantly against U.S. imperialism.

Wherever U.S. imperialism goes--whether in the form of military, political or economic incursions--what inevitably follows is death, poverty and the destruction of cultures, infrastructures and economies.

We stand in solidarity with the people of Africa, Asia, the Middle East, Latin America and beyond, who continue to resist the efforts of imperialist countries to exploit their lands and peoples.

11. Justice and Equality for All Women

Young women are living in a time where the rights that women fought and died to establish are being threatened and, in some states, taken away all together. We demand and end to attacks on women's rights and the establishment of social, economic and sexual equality for all genders and sexes.

We demand reproductive justice for all women including affordable, accessible and safe abortions, full access to safe sex materials and comprehensible funding for childcare.

We must take strides to stop sexual assault and rape. We demand honest and in-depth education about rape and sexual assault for all youth. We demand free recovery programs and counseling, and full legal and financial support for survivors of sexual assault and rape.

We demand equal education for all sexes including equal access, support and encouragement in all classes and extracurricular activities. Campuses need to include anti-sexist trainings for all students.

Abstinence-only-education is preventing schools from teaching all methods of safe sex and from creating programs for young parents.

We demand inclusive sexual education and parenting programs for young parents in every school.

We demand equal pay for equal work, on the job childcare, paid maternity leave and family care days, and comprehensive programs and guidelines to prevent sexual assault on the job.

12. Safety and Equality for lesbian, gay, bi, trans and queer (LGBTQ) youth

We demand an end to the harassment and the verbal, sexual, and physical assault of LGBTQ youth at the hands of police officers. LGBTQ youth are often stopped and forced to present identification to officers, especially if our gender identity and presentation is not that of our assigned gender/sex.

As a result of family disputes and sexual abuse, LGBTQ youth are often likely to be in homeless shelters or living on the streets, where they often have little to no security and support and are even more vulnerable to assault and harassment. We demand funding for safe and accessible community housing for LGBTQ youth. We further demand affordable, accessible, LGBTQ inclusive housing on every campus.

We demand that LGBTQ youth and our allies be free to set up student organizations and events with the full support that any other student group receives. We demand LGBTQ centers on our campuses to provide safe space and resources for LGBTQ youth.

All youth need inclusive and comprehensive sexual education that focuses on the spectrum of sexuality, sex and gender; prevention of sexually transmitted diseases (STDs), sexually transmitted infections (STIs), and youth pregnancy; and teaches about sex in a positive and realistic light.

We demand respectful and adequate healthcare, inclusive health clinics and full health coverage (including hormone treatment, surgery and therapy) for LGBTQ youth. We demand all medical personnel receive LGBTQ inclusive medical training.

We demand job training and placement, anti-discrimination and LGBTQ inclusion trainings for all employees and employers, and legal protections from employee-employee harassment/discrimination.

On the necessity of the fight for a socialist future:

FIST is a youth group that believes the eradication of all forms of oppression and repression is only possible with a revolutionary change in the social relations. While it is important to fight for gains and make material demands on the capitalist government, history has shown that, especially in times of crisis, capitalist governments will always seek to erode demands in the form of social services and that the capitalist class will always seek to take away gains won against them and increase exploitation.

These demands are a platform for struggle, but can ultimately be protected from bourgeois reaction by overthrowing bourgeois society for a socialist future.

Left Hook is the quarterly newspaper of the revolutionary socialist organization for young activists, Fight Imperialism–Stand Together (FIST). Each edition of *Left Hook* will provide analyses of political events, social movements and revolutionary struggles that impact our world. Commentary, theory, culture, and news reporting intersect in the pages of *Left Hook* to provide readers with radical analysis from a Marxist perspective.

Subscribe to *Left Hook*   2 years: $10.00
http://FISTyouth.org

W★RKERS WORLD

We live in a world of fake news. The corporations and big banks that own this so-called media plot overtime to make sure we don't get the truth and fight back. *Workers World* is a different kind of newspaper. Our voices are not those of the status quo or the system's defenders. In WW, you find the voice of workers an oppressed people who strive for a different world in which no one is held down by the chains of exploitation, racism, sexism o anti-LGBT bigotry.

Subscribe to *Workers World* weekly newspaper
workersworld.net
workers.org

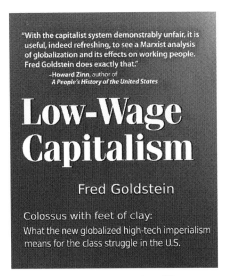

Low-Wage Capitalism

Fred Goldstein

Colossus with feet of clay:
What the new globalized high-tech imperialism
means for the class struggle in the U.S.

Low-Wage Capitalism
What the new globlized high-tech imperialism means for the class struggle in the U.S.

An easy-to-read analysis of the roots of the current global economic crisis, its implications for workers and oppressed peoples, and the strategy needed for future struggle.

"In this period of economic uncertainty, Fred Goldstein's *Low-Wage Capitalism* could not be better timed. Beautifully written, deeply considered and backed by impressive research, this is essential reading for anyone wishing to understand the true nature of the world we live in and the factors that have led to so much turmoil. ... Urgently recommended."
Gregory Elich,
Author of *Strange Liberators*

"We need to get this book into the hands of every worker. It clearly explains the capitalist economic threat to our jobs, our pensions and our homes. But, even more importantly, it shows us how we can fight back and win!"
David Sole, President, UAW Local 2334, Detroit, Michigan

"With the capitalist system demonstrably unfair, irrational, and prone to intermittent crises, it is useful, indeed refreshing, to see a Marxist analysis of globalization and its effects on working people. Fred Goldstein's *Low-Wage Capitalism* does exactly that."
Howard Zinn, author of
*A People's History
of the United States*

"*Low-Wage Capitalism* by Fred Goldstein is a most timely work, as the working class prepares for a fightback during the greatest crisis of capitalism since the Great Depression."
Clarence Thomas, ILWU Local 10 and Co-chair, Million Worker March Movement

"*Low-Wage Capitalism* is truly outstanding. Hits us like a body punch, and provides the perfect context for what we all need to know about the evolving conditions of workers and their struggles. ...
Deserves the widest readership."
Bertell Ollman, author and Professor of Politics, NYU

"Patriarchal prejudice serves capitalism in two ways: it keeps the whole working class divided, and it holds down wages for women and for lesbian, gay, bisexual, and transgendered workers. *Low-Wage Capitalism* shows the necessity and the great potential for solidarity among all the low-wage workers of the world."
Martha Grevatt
Nat'l Executive Officer Pride At Work, AFL-CIO, UAW Local 122

"Lucid, deeply accurate and informative, as relevant and useful as a book can be, Goldstein offers a compelling analysis of the exploitative world of global corporate capitalism. ... "
Michael Parenti,
author of *Contrary Notions*

"160 years after the publication of the *Communist Manifesto*, Fred Goldstein takes on the challenge of applying Marxist political economy to the burgeoning crisis of capitalist globalization in the 21st century. ... "
Abayomi Azikiwe, Editor,
Pan-African News Wire

"From the point of view of Filipino workers in the U.S., the largest exploited and abused Filipino workforce outside the Philippines ... we are pleased with the exposé of imperialist globalization as the main culprit of global forced migration. ... "
Berna Ellorin,
Secretary-General, BAYAN USA

"This book helps us to understand the root of the present neoliberal globalization— a new stage of the international capitalist crisis—which was imposed by U.S. imperialism and which devastated Latin American economies. ...
Ignacio Meneses,
Co-chair, U.S.-Cuba Labor Exchange

World View Forum paperback, 2008, 336 pages, pages, charts, bibliography, index

HIGH TECH, LOW PAY
A Marxist Analysis of the Changing Character of the Working Class
By Sam Marcy, Second Edition with a new introduction by Fred Goldstein

Twenty years ago Marcy wrote that the scientific-technological revolution is accelerating a shift to lower-paying jobs and to more women, Black, Latino/a, Asian, Arab and other nationally oppressed workers.

Using Marxism as a living tool, Marcy analyzes the trends and offers strategies for labor including the occupation of plants

A new introduction by Fred Goldstein, author of *Low-Wage Capitalism*, explains the roots of the current economic crisis, with its disastrous unemployment, which has heightened the need for a working-class resurgence.

World View Forum paperback, 2009, 156 pages, charts, bibliography, index

Books available online at **Leftbooks.com** and on sale at bookstores around the country.

Rainbow Solidarity
In Defense of
CUBA

By Leslie Feinberg

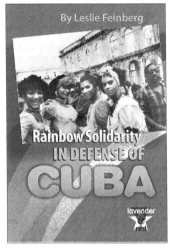

By Leslie Feinberg author of
Stone Butch Blues

Rainbow Solidarity in Defense of Cuba
documents revolutionary Cuba's inspiring trajectory of progress towards liberation of sexualities, genders and sexes.

This ground-breaking book reveals how the Cuban Revolution has grappled with the pre-revolutionary legacy of 450 years of persecution and exploitation of homosexuality.

Rainbow Solidarity answers the demonization of the 1959 Cuban Revolution by Washington and the CIA, Wall Street and Hollywood by demonstrating that the process of solving these problems is the forward motion of the revolution.

Today, after decades of concrete efforts and achievements—together with free health care and education, and jobs and housing for all— Cubans enjoy freedoms regarding same-sex love, transsexuality and gender expression in Cuba that don't exist in the imperialist United States.

 Rainbow Solidarity in Defense of Cuba is an edited compilation of 25 articles from the *Workers World* newspaper series by Feinberg entitled Lavender & Red, online at www.workers.org

World View Forum paperback 2008, 116 pages, photos, bibliography, index

First public event for Rainbow Solidarity for the Cuban Five at the New York City LGBT Community Center in June 2007. Secretary Jorge Luis Dustet from the United Nations Cuban Mission he holds up poster with the names of the first 1,000 signers of the call for Rainbow Solidarity with the Cuban Five.

The Cuban Five are Gerardo Hernández Nordelo, Ramón Labañino Salazar, Rene González Sehwerert, Antonio Guerrero Rodríguez and Fernando González Llort, political prisoners held in U.S. prisions.

MARXISM, REPARATIONS
& the Black Freedom Struggle

An anthology of writings from *Workers World* newspaper.
Edited by Monica Moorehead. Includes:

Racism, National Oppression
and Self-Determination
Larry Holmes

Black Labor from Chattel Slavery
to Wage Slavery
Sam Marcy

Harriet Tubman, Woman Warrior
Mumia Abu-Jamal

Black Youth: Repression & Resistance
LeiLani Dowell

Black & Brown Unity:
A Pillar of Struggle for Human Rights
and Global Justice!
Saladin Muhammad

Are Conditions Ripe Again Today?
40th Anniversary of the 1965
Watts Rebellion
John Parker

Racism and Poverty in the Delta
Larry Hales

The Struggle for Socialism Is Key
Monica Moorehead

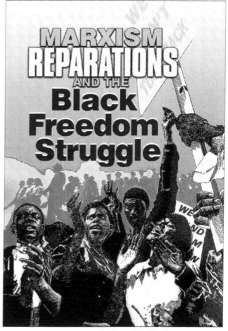

COVER ILLUSTRATION BY SAHU BARRON

Domestic Workers United Demand
Passage of a Bill of Rights
Imani Henry

Causes of Turmoil in Jamaica
Pat Chin

Africa Needs Reparations,
Not Occupation and Sanctions
Deirdre Griswold

Black Reconstruction:
The Unfinished Revolution
Minnie Bruce Pratt

World View Forum 2007, paperback
200 pages, photos

"These essays, from a variety of folks working on a number of Black struggles, testify to the central truth that Black History is the epic saga of resistance, rebellion and revolt. These struggles show us all that true freedom is still an objective to be attained, rather than a reality. What, pray tell, did Katrina show us?"

— Mumia Abu-Jamal
Political prisoner writing from
Pennsylvania's death row. His 6th book published by City Lights Books, 2009
*Jailhouse Lawyers: Prisoners
Defending Prisoners vs. the U.S.A.*
is available at Leftbooks.com.

Books available online at **Le*f*tbooks.com** and on sale at bookstores around the country.

A Voice from Harper's Ferry, 1859
by Osborne P. Anderson, a Black revolutionary who was there.

Also the essays

The Neglected Voices from Harper's Ferry
Mumia Abu-Jamal

What Is a Nation?
Monica Moorehead

The Unfinished Revolution
Vince Copeland

A unique book from the raid on Harper's Ferry. Few history books give Osborne P. Anderson the recognition he deserves. Anderson was the only Black combatant to survive the raid and to write about it. His account of this turning point in the struggle against slavery—an armed attack by Black and white volunteers on a citadel of the South—refutes those who try to minimize the role of African American people in fighting for their freedom.

World View Forum paperback,
124 pages, photos

The Prison-Industrial Complex:
An interview with Mumia Abu-Jamal

Monica Moorehead and Larry Holmes interview Mumia—journalist, political activist and wrongfully convicted death row inmate —framed for his ideas. Abu-Jamal speaks on prison labor in the United States, youth, elections, economics and the state of the world.

Also includes articles on:

The Oppressed Nations, the Poor & Prisons
Monica Moorehead

The Death Penalty & the Texas Killing Machine
Teresa Gutierrez

World View Forum, 2000
paperback, saddle stitched,
32 pages, photos

Books available online at *Leftbooks.com* and on sale at bookstores around the country.

Made in the USA